Once There Was
a Passenger Pigeon

By Esther S. and Bernard L. Gordon

ONCE
THERE WAS
A PASSENGER
PIGEON

Pictures by Lawrence Di Fiori

HENRY Z. WALCK, INC.
New York

*The authors wish to acknowledge the assistance
rendered by Toni Strassman, Lorna Greenberg and
Joseph Gordon in the preparation of this book.*

Library of Congress Cataloging in Publication Data
Gordon, Esther S
    Once there was a passenger pigeon.
    SUMMARY: A description and history of the
passenger pigeon of North America, once one of the
world's most numerous birds, but, due to thoughtless
killing, now extinct.
    1. Passenger pigeons—Juvenile literature.
[1. Passenger pigeons] I. Gordon, Bernard L.,
joint author. II. Di Fiori, Lawrence.
III. Title.
QL696.C63G67   598.6'1   75–37484
ISBN 0–8098–5003–6

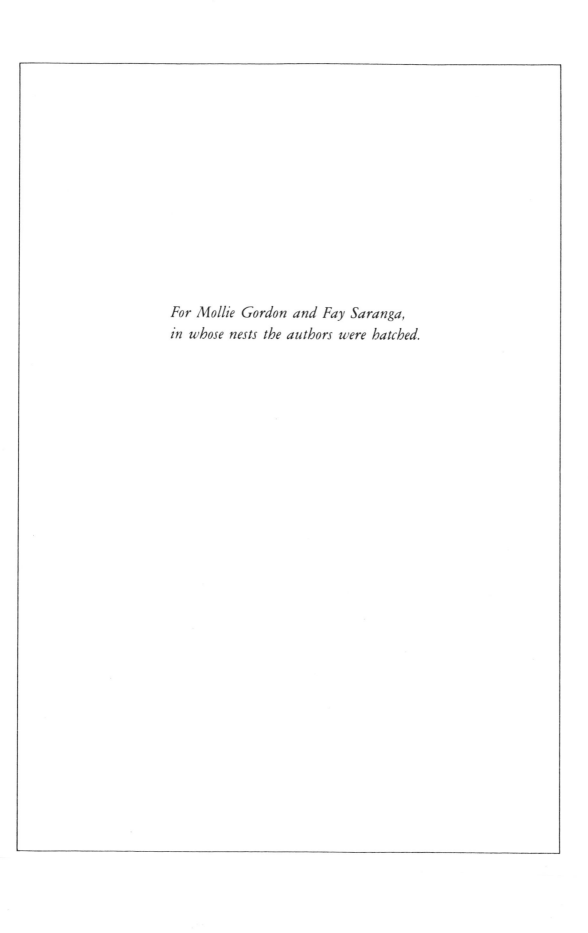

For Mollie Gordon and Fay Saranga,
in whose nests the authors were hatched.

ONCE the passenger pigeon or wild pigeon of North America was one of the world's most numerous birds. In the eighteenth and nineteenth centuries there were billions of these beautiful birds in the United States and Canada.

In 1625, Nicholoes van Wassenaer, a Dutch historian who was visiting the settlement at New Amsterdam (where New York City now is), wrote that there were so many pigeons that they darkened the skies, completely shutting out the sunshine. Today, not a single passenger pigeon is alive. The species is no more —it is extinct.

The last wild passenger pigeon was killed in 1906 in Connecticut. And the last living passenger pigeon, a bird named Martha, died at the Cincinnati, Ohio, Zoo in 1914.

The birds were described as "pigeons of passage" by Mark Catesby in 1743, and their Latin name *Ectopistes migratorius* means migratory wanderers. Every spring great flocks of these pigeons migrated from the southern states to breeding grounds in colder areas of the United States and Canada. Here, they nested and raised their young. When the summer ended, the flocks—with their newly hatched birds—headed south again for the winter.

In 1808, Alexander Wilson, a Scottish-born American bird authority, saw a flock near Frankfort, Kentucky, flying toward Indiana. He estimated the flock to be a mile wide and 240 miles long. This he calculated would be 2,230,272,000 birds, or over two billion passenger pigeons in one flock! He figured they would eat about 434,000 bushels of acorns, rice, nuts, berries and grain each day.

John James Audubon, America's most famous bird artist, made careful studies of passenger pigeons near the Ohio River in the fall of 1813. He wrote that the air was so filled with pigeons, it seemed as if the sun were in eclipse. Bird droppings fell like snowflakes. When a hawk approached the flock, the birds quickly grouped together, their wings making a noise like thunder. Then the flock moved on in a winding curve, like a giant snake.

Audubon also noted that the pigeons could fly swiftly over great distances. Pigeons killed near New York City still had food pouches or crops full of rice. The nearest rice fields were in the Carolinas and Georgia. Since the food would be digested in twelve hours, the birds must have traveled from the southern coastal plains in about half a day, or as fast as a mile a minute, or sixty miles an hour!

The passenger pigeon was one of the largest and most beautiful members of the pigeon family. It was different from the pigeons we see today. It was about eighteen inches long. It had a long graceful neck, a slender bill and legs, and narrow streamlined wings. Its tail was eight inches long, with twelve feathers that were silvery white on their undersides. The upper part of the wings and the back and head were dark blue, and looked velvety. The neck was gold and green mixed with royal purple, and the breast was reddish brown. The female was about an inch shorter than the male, and its feathers were not as bright.

The pigeon flocks were often noisy and made sounds like the croaking of wood frogs. They also clucked, shrieked, chattered and cooed, usually creating a loud din.

When a flock of passenger pigeons roosted, they covered acres of forest. A male and a female bird would build a nest together, using dry slender twigs. One egg was laid in the nest.

There were nests in all the trees in the area —the pines, the hemlocks, the oaks, the maples and any others. Large trees might have as many as ninety nests, each seven or more feet above the ground. The weight of so many nests sometimes broke the branches, and ruined the forest for miles around.

Overhead, hawks and eagles soared, looking for chances to snatch a tasty pigeon. On the ground, foxes, lynxes, cougars, bears, opossums and polecats gathered, hoping to catch a stray squab that had tumbled from its nest. These predators were always on the lookout for pigeons which might stray from the flocks.

The newly hatched birds were fed pigeon milk by both their parents. This food was made in the upper end of the pigeon's digestive tract, called the crop. It smelled like cheese, and was similar to the milk of mammals. The nestlings received nothing but the pigeon milk for their first three days; then they began to eat grain and seeds mixed with pigeon milk.

After a month the nestlings weighed almost a pound and were called squabs. The young squabs were fat and tasty, and were eagerly hunted. They brought good prices at markets. Hunters and trappers pulled or pushed the squabs out of the nests with wooden poles. Sometimes they chopped down trees to get the young birds.

In May, 1880, Chief Simon Pokagon of the Pokagon Indians visited the last known nesting place of the passenger pigeon east of Lake Michigan, on the Platt River. Large white birch trees were filled with nests. The Indian chief saw how cruel the hunters were to the young birds. They set fire to the trees to force the clumsy young birds to leap to the ground, while the parent birds flew up to escape the flames. Chief Pokagon also saw farmers set out wheat soaked in whiskey. After eating it, the birds would lose their balance or become unconscious, and could be easily captured.

Hunters and trappers slaughtered billions of passenger pigeons. As many as 5,000 birds were caught in a single day by one trapper using a net in a good location. Over a billion passenger pigeons were caught by trappers in one season in 1878. They used large net traps, sulfur fumes and poisonous gases, snares and shotguns.

Some trappers used "stool pigeons" to lure flying birds down to the ground. The "stool pigeon" was a bird with its eyelids sewn closed, and tied to a wooden stool. From a hiding place, the trapper used a long pole to control the stool. When a flock of pigeons appeared, the hunter raised and lowered the stool causing the stool pigeon to flutter, flap its wings and land. This action lured the flock to a nearby field that was baited with corn and grain. A huge net hung from poles would be dropped onto the feeding birds, trapping hundreds at a time.

Pigeons sold for thirty-five to forty cents a dozen at the traps. In Chicago markets, they sold for fifty cents a dozen. Young pigeons brought twelve cents a dozen in the woods. Live birds were more valuable, and sold for one to two dollars a dozen in the large cities.

Live pigeons were also used as targets at shooting contests. One three-day Bird Shoot Contest held in 1899 at Elkwood Park, New Jersey, attracted 266 competitors who killed 20,000 pigeons.

Thoughtless killing doomed this lovely bird. Conservationists were slow in trying to save it. In 1848 the state of Massachusetts passed a law that protected the *netters* of wild pigeons from interference. The law also provided for a fine of ten dollars for those who damaged pigeon nets or frightened the birds away. Killing wild pigeons was a profitable industry.

The first law to protect wild pigeons was passed by New York State in 1867. Massachusetts followed in 1870, and forbade killing the pigeons except during a hunting season. But it was already late and the sad end of the passenger pigeon was very near. Nobody listened to the warnings of the conservationists.

The last wild passenger pigeon was captured near Detroit, Michigan, on September 14, 1908. Many zoos had live passenger pigeons on display in 1900. The Cincinnati Zoological Gardens had descendants of a small flock of wild pigeons that had been brought from Shawano County, Wisconsin, in 1879. But one by one the captive birds died. In 1910 only an old male and female were left alive in all the world. These two passenger pigeons were carefully protected with the hope that they would produce eggs and new birds. But, alas, this did not happen. The male died of old age in 1910 and Martha, the last living passenger pigeon in the world, died at about the age of twenty-nine on September 1, 1914. Pigeon authorities say the age of twenty years in pigeons is equal to the age of ninety years in human beings. So Martha was a very old bird.

Martha was preserved and protected for posterity. Her body was mounted and stuffed and placed in a glass case at the Smithsonian Institution in Washington, D.C. The following label appears on the display

Ectopistes migratorius (Linnaeus)
Passenger Pigeon
Exterminated. Formerly very abundant through-
out a large part of North America. This is the
last known individual. It died in captivity in
September, 1914.

Today, other birds are threatened with extinction. The whooping crane, the osprey or fish hawk, the bald eagle, the snowy egret, the Florida Everglade kite, the Kirtland warbler, the California condor, the prairie chicken and the sandhill crane are all in danger. And there are others. Some are being destroyed by sportsmen, others by plume hunters who seek colorful feathers, and still others by our use of chemical pesticides. We need national and state bird sanctuaries, conservation laws, the teaching of wildlife protection and a ban on the use of poisonous insecticides. Only then will we be able to save our endangered animals from the cruel fate of the bird whose wings produced thunder over the plains and forests of America, and whose numbers darkened the skies—the vanished passenger pigeon.